A HANDFUL OF LIFE

BOOK OF POETRY

Written By
ANDREA WARDSWORTH BEASLEY

TABLE OF CONTENTS

TABLE OF CONTENTS

TABLE OF CONTENTS

INTRODUCTION

WELCOME to "A HANDFUL OF LIFE BOOK OF POEMS!" Glimpse my "Poetic Journey" through the tapestry of Life's Existence. In this Collection of Poems, each verse unveils the intricate threads of life such as moments of joy, whispers of sorrow, and the dance between the light, the shadows, and the dark! These Poems, like the reflections in a multifaceted mirror, explore the diverse facets of Human experiences. From the tender embrace of love to the resilient rise from challenges, and solitude this anthology weaves emotions into verses, inviting you to explore the profound beauty found in every corner of existence. You will find and read poetry about the echoes of children, moms, dads, cousins, and other family members that may resonate with your own everyday Life and Spirit. Join me as we wander through the symphony of "A Handful of Life Book of Poems" savoring the richness found in the diversity of the Life verses, one-moments, one-emotions, one-poem and finally one-story at a time.

"WE ARE BORN FOR THIS DAY!"

We are all in the Family of "Human Being"! Our Nation is only as strong as our Families are. We are a daily display of Faith. We are learning to follow the leading of the Holy Spirit. We are seeking, seeing, and reaping the great benefits of His guide. Children usually follow the example of their parents. As adults, we do pass on a family blessing and/or a family curse. There are "Sins of the Fathers" that can pass on from past generations to present generations. Children reared obedient through the love and respect of others; especially from the example made of their parents is a good thing. We must build better relationships and assume responsibility to care for one another in both the good times and bad times, whether you are rich, or poor. Every Family has their own troubles, but one of God's greatest resources is the FAMILY.

Jesus has made the way to adopt us all into the Family of God. One faithful parent can impact the world starting right in your own home with the family God has given you." Why not start with YOU? I pray that you expect many more signs, wonders and miracles now more than ever before in your life and mine! I introduce this Book of Poetry with my Poem entitled.....
" A Handful of Life!"

A HANDFUL OF LIFE

In my palm, a Handful of Life unfolds,
A tapestry of stories, a saga to be told.
Each moment held, a gem in my hand,
A mosaic of joy, like grains of sand.

Laughter sparkles, a radiant hue,
Glistening like dewdrops in morning's view.
Challenges faced, lessons learned,
In this Handful of Life, wisdom earned.

Love's embrace, a warmth so sweet,
Binding hearts in a rhythm complete.
Adventures woven in the fabric of time,
A handful of life, so sublime.

Tears may fall like gentle rain,
Washing away the transient pain,
Yet in this grasp, resilience springs,
A Handful of Life, with myriad wings.

Hold it gently, this fleeting grace,
Time's caress in a finite space.
In the palm of now, let stories thrive,

For in a Handful of Life, we truly are ALIVE!

ACKNOWLEDMENTS

In the tapestry of verses, gratitude does unfold
To those whose presence, like my stories told

To the muse that whispered, unseen and always near
"A Handful of Life", your essence I revere

To friends and family steadfast and to me so true,
Your support and love, whether it be many or few

To the readers who wander through these ephemeral stages

May you find solace in these life's divine and diverse pages.

"Catch the ball and run with it!"

~Thank you~

ANDREA'S TESTIMONY

"I am a blessed woman of God!" I stand on this scripture: It is written, (NIV) 2 Corinthians 9:8. "And my God makes all grace abound towards me and every favor and Earthly blessing, so that I have sufficiency in all things and abound in every good work." It has been ten years now since my five children, and I were in a House Fire that consumed everything that we owned at two o'clock one October morning. We walked away down that dark street well and thanked God for our lives. I was a single divorced parent and teacher at that time. I remember praying to God the very night before our House Fire in the bathroom of our rented house, asking God to help us, as I cried out to him upset with our past life, or the "Handful of Life" that I had been dealt. I did not ever understand why it was taking SO, SO very long to bring MY Family to our "Place of MORE Prosperity", as I was doing ALL I knew to do to provide and be a good mom and wife. I was also nice to others. During these times we needed to move on and live a better LIFE. Many a day I only had ONE DOLLAR bill left in my purse, or just the coin change from my only monthly school paycheck. I was struggling financially ALL the time! I worked two to three jobs; one as a special education teacher, one part-time job at Sears, and one part-time job as a Counselor trying to provide necessities, food, entertainment, and activities for my kids. We received one hundred dollars a month in child support for five children and FOUGHT to get that! My comment was, "What the Hell!" One week after that Fire, our temporary needs were met with clothes, food, and money with my church's and the community's help for a month. The Life & Styles TV Show contacted me through a news article written in the Alexandria Daily Town Talk about the Fire. I assumed that being on The Life & Styles Show would provide me with some relaxation, but I still had to work hard! Decisions had to be made regarding what to wear, what to do, what to do with my hair, and so forth, as they picked us up an hour after the airplane landed to handle those details. **10**

That experience and the change of scenery in that City was such a good eye-opening experience, as I had never been to New York. The City was very cold and full of snow. I would love the chance to revisit in late spring one more time. I continued to pray and believe in God. We were able to buy five acres of land with the intentions to build a new family home, build a gravel road for the property, and help buy a used car for my oldest son who had started working at fifteen years of age at a gas station on the corner of Jackson Street to help himself survive. We continued to believe in God for our house to be built, but it was too hard to share that vision with the neighboring banks. They wanted to use their builder contractors with the money they agreed to lend me, but that would NOT do for my needs, especially after I had completed all the legwork to find my building supplies and own contractors myself! We bought an existing house seven years later. I was inspired to start baking cakes, and making pear preserves, and started a test market for these items for a family business; ZONA'S PLACE. Then, I was inspired to start designing yard signs used for outreach into the community for our church members – to "See, Hear, and Feel the Love of God at the Word Christian Center Church!" That was my motto on the signs I made and printed for The Word Christian Center Church Members who were interested. As God led and inspired me, I kept nurturing HIS sacred ideas and wrote them down until I stepped out on Faith.

I was sitting in the rocking chair reading my Bible and this Scripture jumped out at me; John 15:5-14 (NIV) Jesus said, "I am the vine." No branch can bear fruit unless I remain in YOU. Apart from Him I can do nothing. I may ask what I wish, and it will be given to me. It is my Father's glory that I bear much fruit... showing myself to be his disciple. My Heavenly Father was telling me to surrender ALL! The pieces would eventually come together. He had already died for me. He brought me out of the FIRE already.

...So OUR NEW LIFE has begun again.
...Here I am today!   11

GREETINGS!

Philippians 1 (NIV)

Every time I think of you, I give thanks to my God. 4 Whenever I pray, I make my requests for all of you with joy, 5 for you have been my partners in spreading the Good News about Christ from the time you first heard it until now. 6 And I am certain that God, who began the good work within you, will continue his work until it is finally finished on the day when Christ Jesus returns.

7 So it is right that I should feel as I do about all of you, for you have a special place in my heart. You share with me the special favor of God, both in my imprisonment and in defending and confirming the truth of the Good News. 8 God knows how much I love you and long for you with the tender compassion of Christ Jesus.

9 I pray that your love will overflow more and more and that you will keep on growing in knowledge and understanding. 10 For I want you to understand what matters, so that you may live pure and blameless lives until the day of Christ's return. 11 May you always be filled with the fruit of your salvation—the righteous character produced in your life by Jesus Christ [11] —for this will bring much glory and praise to God.

~Much love, Andrea and Children~

12

A LETTER TO MY PRESIDENT AND MRS OBAMA
(Written and Mailed to White House in January 2009)

Dear Mr. President & Mrs. Obama,

CONGRATULATIONS to you both for your continued terms of service to our Nation! "Life has been squeezing our lemons in Louisiana, but I still want to share some good Country Time Lemonade with friends like you!"

Although, it costs us to work, we must maintain an active status of staying employed in this present economy. Many of us have struggled financially for years, so this is "OUR TIME" to get Middle Class America OUT of poverty and lack. When the hurricanes and floods come here, many are denied access to reasonable loans and insurance and other assistance for day-to-day living, yet Louisiana remains a "Happy State"! This is my Home!

I appreciate First Lady Obama being an advocate, role model, and voice to many other women and young girls who have many God-given dreams, ideas, and talents that need to be exposed. I will continue to put my hands to the plow. I sow into good ground, and we are ready to reap our great benefits and harvest today from your Leadership. We do not give up. We shall continue to press forward! ...."Yes, WE Can!"

In closing, I thank you, Mr. President and Mrs. Obama, for your time and consideration given to the citizens of Nation. Again, I thank God for giving you the ability and wisdom to help lead and unite this Nation, as you help restore it's people to where God intended them to be:

One Nation under GOD!

Sincerely,
Andrea Wardsworth Baker and the Family

THE CHILDREN'S PLACE

Life is precious…

It feels like holding water or sand slipping through your fingers!

Move Ahead. Explore your dreams.

Ask questions. Continue to learn and grow.
Create your own intrigue.

Life is Meaningful…

You must make it last while it lasts!

~~~~~~~~~~~~~~~~~~~

THE CHILDREN'S PLACE

God did give us ALL a measure of hopes, dreams, blessings, and our quiver of children to raise, teach, love, and share things with; whether adopted or biological! HE controls everything to save our Souls. It is up to us to step out on Faith and pass on the Generational Blessings and Pride to the hearts of our Family. I use THIS writing Space to speak into their lives and your children's lives as well; should YOU find my voice favorable. We each have a special part. The Poems written here in..... The Children's Place are writings by my children that I saved when they were very young, spanning from the second to sixth grades. My gifted children all have talents to create, dream, build, write, and take leadership. Pay attention to YOUR Children. They were ALL academic Honor Students who excelled and stayed disciplined in School. This fact was simply a MIRACLE to Me in itself! Yes, I am a VERY Proud MOM! All of my children had THEIR problems like most others without a Full-time father figure in the household, and WE overcame and are still overcoming some obstacles. I continue to reach out to my Heavenly Father for help through Prayer and Counsel on my children's behalf with a Mother's Heart! I also received help from my Parents, especially my Mother, Sister, other Mothers, Soccer Moms, and Friends while raising my kids from babies to young adults. I sincerely thank you ALL again so much for your HELP with MY CHILDREN and Thank You, GOD, My Heavenly Father! Read and Write to Your Children. These activities will help them GROW!

F-A-T-H-E-R

F or all things you've attempted to talk us through
A nd for telling us that you are here for us and love us too
T hrough and through we do see our hopes replaced
H elping us with anything, and everything we have faced
E very day you're there for us by simply calling us to check-in
R arely do we thank you enough before our day will begin
So on this special day we do exactly that; we say thank you, as
    we speak to the "seen and unseen"
            "Thank you for being our F A T H E R!"   14

The First Son

My first son was given his Dad's first name being the first-born son to a lineage of three generations of males with the same first name in that Family. His birth took fourteen hours! I thought I was dying birthing him, but I did learn from each birth thereafter! God is not through with him. This son was dreaming during the House Fire. The flames had engulfed his room to a crisp; all except the bed he was sleeping in! Later on, he informed us that he was dreaming! He was trying to help lead a young man from a devil and the guy had just barely made it in through the opened door in time from the devil's sharp hooked knife. He has had trials, and he knows the power of prayer. He is so smart, loves finer things, and loves routine. He has always been so naturally knowledgeable about life, disciplined with work, and always very loved by others. Many would tell me they are impressed with him because he is helpful, and mannerable despite some setbacks! My first son served in the Navy and was named a blessed thinker and doer! He is a friendly handsome young man and he respects elders! He has compassion and faith in God. He has a knack for Entrepreneurship! Obedience will always be the key for him to stay in his anointed leadership position and natural progression to becoming another "King David" amongst men. It only takes that one anointed stone to knock down and slay any giant in your Life, Son! God is so good! Stand and stay the course. God will cause you to have great success! You are such a kind Spirit. "Make your next TOUCHDOWN WITH LIFE!   .....Love Mom

----

Writings by First Son

"Mamma, Mamma, Mamma!"

"Mamma, Mamma, Mamma, Mama---ee, Mam—ee! "Mamma come see!" Mamma, can you fix me some cereal?" ...Please?

Mamma, can you buy me something? These are all the favorite words spoken all day long by the five children of Andrea Marie Wardsworth.

Our Mom is also a Teacher professionally. She works hard at trying to keep her students motivated to learn and stay in school. She is also an active Club Sponsor of the Natural Helpers Club at Peabody Magnet High School. This Club does things for the Community and allows us to take field trips! She brings books home and searches the Internet to find activities for her students almost daily. Mom has to check and grade student papers, find time to read for herself, take us places, get food to cook us something to eat, and entertain us. I asked her to find another job that would make more money because she has a lot to do as a Teacher and care for us. There never seems to be enough money or time to support us all.

On top of this, we had that house fire, which added to the work our Mom had to do. My Mom just kept on going with all of us. She has kept herself going. I do not see how she does it! She deserves some time off and a day to herself. I do not know where we would be without her. I know that she has a strong belief in GOD. Can you imagine yourself or us five without a MOM? We want to say,

"We Love You, Mom!"

THE NIGHTMARE THAT CAME TRUE

THE FIRE

"You have no authority you devil; I am covered in the Blood."
"Yeah, take that now! You know that I am loved."

I sleep so peacefully only to awaken to my worst nightmare.
A house fire of great proportion, smoke here and smoke over
    there.
I heard, "Get up Lex, the house is on FIRE!"
Half asleep, I did not even know what my brother was talking
    about that was so dire.

I did not realize it then, but I soon found out.
"What in the world is that smell? Oh no, it's smoke. No
    doubt, Get out!"

All I knew was one thing...grab my Jordan tennis shoes and
    Go. Go, Go so I would not choke!
My Mom yells, "I need my purse, but there is so much
    smoke!"

I ran back inside the house to see if I could find my mother's
    possession.
I did not care about any diminishing air obsession.

I returned from our flaming house with no such luck.
Now I realized that I was truly, "One Brave Young Buck."

Black, smoke smeared, and burnt were now the words, that
    characterized our house on the news.
That afternoon all I could think was... "MY SHOES!"

God gave me the strength to show my face the next day at
    school!
That house fire had no golden rules!

The Second Son

It took me three days to name my son. He seemed to glisten as I looked upon his face. He reminded me so much of God's bright light. I soon realized after my first child that your BIRTH NAME is very very important, so I did not want to do him an injustice; as he is another gift from God. Yes, he is! Then, his name came to me--- He was a joy and had a very high-pitched streaking cry that could be heard throughout the house when he was a baby. His hands and long outstretched fingers were strong. His skinny legs were also so long. His mind was so alert with eyes that seemed to scan his surroundings in the room yet, his voice was scarcely heard as a young child, nor throughout his teen years when it was time for him to talk. He would not talk much. He later became known as the rebounding "Ghost", the "Gentle Giant", and the "BMW" both on and off the basketball court with his academic honors and achievements in his high school class. My second son is tall and handsome. Everything from the top of his head to the soul of his feet is blessed. He seemed to thrive with being creative and loved to work his mind and hands. He reminds me of Nehemiah and Joseph in the Bible. He is a leader, builder, and fixer. He is a great listener, dedicated worker, and provider! My son has compassion and faith in God! Walk in your greatness and continue to "SLAM DUNK WITH LIFE!"

.....Love Mom.

Writings by Second Son

FIRE

The intense heat of red to blue hue.

INTENSE

Intense heat of orange to red hue
Flames of yellow and blue
All consumed in its path
Faith only does I hath

A FACE OF PERIL

In the shadows of the night, where nightmares unfold,
I awoke to a tale of fire and a hero untold.
The crackling whispers of danger near,
A dance of flames, and awakening fear.

The stench of burnt marshmallows and smoke filled the air,
Silent sirens echoed in my heart knowing danger was near.
As I sprang to life, urging everyone to wake as the smoke swirls,
For my mother and siblings, are the center of my world.

In the hush of embers, Mom screams grab what we can,
For the memories in that home won't ever be seen again.
A lullaby of danger, a flickering song
Who knew a strong family is what we had all along?

God touched us, as he guided our escapes,
In the face of peril, we found our capes.
From the streets we watched, in our minds uncertainty resides,
At least we were safe, standing side by side.

Tender hands grasped in the cloak of night,
A family's bond, a beacon of light.
Through the ashes we emerged, in all our entire,
A tale of awakening and escaping the fire!

FIRE IN THE NIGHT

Pitch black with not much to see,

A strange stench approaches me,

The smell grew louder as the suspense grew,

Oh, what should one in my predicament do?

Check the hall and check the kitchen,

Next, the room where the light does glisten,

Smoke fills the air and burns my eyes,

What is this light next to the bed where my family lies?

Get up! Get up! I scream in fear,

Everyone needs to get out of here,

Sizzle and crackle the fire roars,

Grasp what you can and sprint to the doors,

Into the night sky, we escape in luck,

What if I would not have woken up?

This would cause everything to go amuck!

I stand and watch as the flames destroy the lumber,

Of what was once my home and place of slumber?

The Third Son

My third son was named after the biblical Hebrew King and is a "Warrior Boss". As I watched him grow, and after he had his first accident cutting his leg from the table glass, I knew that he was also like "Sampson" in the Bible because he was growing tall, thick, and so strong, yet still with such a childlike, and playful nature without realizing his strength. This son looks more like an Indian. He has a smooth olive complexion like the American Indians we all are. My middle outspoken son needed to establish his territory amongst his older brothers. He also wanted and claimed his youth amongst the two younger siblings. In other words, he would side with his two older siblings to act more mature, then switch to the more immature side with his two younger siblings, just like a true middle child. Therefore, he is the exact "middle" of both worlds! He is one whom I know without a shadow of a doubt that his destiny is only in God's Hands regarding any personal battles, and he does well with routine. Usually, he tries to figure things out on his own as he makes mistakes, but God has his hands on him and will always strengthen him during each trial. He loved playing baseball. My son learns patience daily and obtains a deeper vision of Life each day. He has grown and will be a mighty force for the "Good" and a mighty force to reckon with in the future, as his greater future successes are ahead, and God will bring him into that Place of Abundance! God will help you establish great things and relationships now! Continue to trust HIM and make your "GRAND SLAM WTH LIFE!"   .....Love Mom.

Writings by the Third Son

WHAT IS FIRE?

The sight of fire
Has no desire
Fire kills, destroys, and burns
But with God
One has no concern

A Wandering Mind

The mind is full of imagination
The world is full of sin and temptation
A wondering mind had no destination
So get off your procrastination

High On Life

The moon rises and the sun sets
I am high off life and drunk off success.

The stars shine the clouds float
When God comes I want to be on that boat

The Planets orbit in the universe
I am a blessing and not a curse

My One and Only Daughter

My daughter is a precious, amazing, beautiful, talented Honor Student with two degrees! What would I do without her? I shall not even think about that question for more than a second! She is a Boss too! I wanted to be blessed with a daughter, then she was born! Glory to GOD! I am still so excited about that! I compare her to Queen Ester in the Bible.

Before she was born, I heard her name whispered to me as I sat on the couch in the living room. Her name traveled to me on the sound of a small whistling wind. I heard she would "sing like a songbird" one day. (We shall see when that happens. It may be through her poems and story writings because she is so good at writing!)

My Daughter loves listening to music and has become quite artistic by designing her crafts during her spare time. She excels in whatever she does. She wants to establish a business enterprise and listens to God on her own.

She has beautiful thick curly hair and is truly GIFTED! One day she, my Soror Sister Daughter will realize truly gifted she is, and her true worth. "You Go Girl!" Learn to play your guitar, you are a Shining Star!

My only daughter possesses remarkable insight, intellect, and character strength. She is truly a gold five-star Indian girl beauty who cherishes nature and the land. She strengthens our Family by fostering close bonds among her brothers, each with their unique personalities! Her creative talents, strategic planning and thinking shine through in both her plans and our Family goals, especially in times of adversity. She is wise, dependable, and deeply faithful!
I could go on and on. My Daughter, stay your course and do not overthink, or worry about anything! Enjoy your Life!

I pray for your excellent GOD-GIVEN Husband to cross your path now also! You are such a delightful person. I truly do appreciate having you as my Daughter! So, Brothers I need you to watch over your Sister! Protect your Sister and check in with her always.

Okay My Daughter, name your tune, then MAKE YOUR MARK WITH LIFE!

.........Love Mom

A World of Fire

My world is burning down
As the flames rise higher
Sadness can always be found
In the destruction of fire

Life

Life is full of tragedy and surprises
Some days are filled with sorrow
No one can hide it
I cannot wait until tomorrow
Maybe tomorrow things will change
Maybe tomorrow things just won't
No one can stop the pain
Trying to does not mean people don't
You never know what tomorrow brings
 It may be good or bad
There are some hurtful things
That can make you very sad
But life is not all wrong
You just have to keep on moving along

MA

Ma was trustworthy. She meant a lot to me.
She was my friend and my Great Grandmother.
She raised my Mother when she was little.
She told me how life was back then.
She said that candy cost five cents a pound to spend.
She made me laugh. She made me smile.
I loved her cause she would play with me a while.
I would help braid her hair.
She knew that I would always care.
Now, she is gone, and I am very sad. I was never bad.
 I miss her.

THE MEMORY OF YOU

Sleepless nights, lonely days

The memory of you is just a haze

The way I feel...it is not a phase

My life right now is just a maze

Getting through it is what I crave

Without any hurt, without any pain

Sleepless nights, lonely days

The memory of you is just a haze

TRAGIC HERO

You made me feel as if I could fly
You gave me the strength I did not know I had
You told me I could conquer whatever I believed in

And I did
And I believed in us

You made me a hero
A beautiful and tragic hero
But my fatal flaw was believing we wouldn't reach our downfall

THE ARTIST'S DEPARTURE
(Written in Memory of Grandaddy Anderson "Chico")

If I described your life, I would use the word "art" because you were a
piece of work
The most vibrant colors seem to fade the fastest and you were the most
colorful person I knew

But you were more than artwork, you were an artist, too
Your wife, Mary, stayed by your side and guided your strokes with a steady
hand
She always made sure your colors were blended well and cleaned your
dirty brushes as well as she could
She was your perfect complement

If your children were paintings, they'd be the greatest work you've ever
created
You painted Andrea in golds and kindness
Bathed her in earth tones and outlined her mindset in bold
You created Anna with jewel tones and compassion
Lathered her in the color of the sunset and etched her spirit with airy lines
Later, You crafted your grandchildren from the hues of a rainbow and
gave a new name to every color

And even though you are gone we can still visualize the imprint you've left
on our lives
So we will fill you in
And You will surround us

From your memory we will make mountains and from your laugher we
will create oceans
Trees will speak of your accomplishments
Valleys will remember your name
Soon Flowers will bloom for you
And the sky will become your home
And when we are finished, we will sign it "Love"

Your art touched souls and kissed spirits
So It didn't matter how big your canvas was
It was never about the length or the height
Because everyone who had a chance to witness this
Masterpiece loved you so much more deeply

THE SKY IS THE LIMIT?

Why do people say the sky is the limit?
When people have already been to the moon
Not many minds can fully understand this
But life ends too soon
So, hope for the good
But expect the bad
Do as you should
And always look ahead

SIMILAR

Some people might not figure out writing
Some might not understand life

They are similar
They can both be shortened or grow
They can wither away or be renewed
They can change

I AM GLASS

I am filled with sorrow and sadness
I try not to cry
I tremble
I am glass
And I am about to break

BITTER SWEET

I have to look back
All the lessons I have learned
Some bitter
Some sweet
All important
I am thankful

FUN AND GAMES

I see scratches on my life
And the thorns that caused them
This is not a game
It is not Hide-n-Seek
I wish it was
Then, I could start over.

WONDERFUL WEATHER

Skies are blue
Grass is green
It is cool outside
The air is crisp
The sun is warm
The clouds are like cotton
Trees sway
Birds sing
Wonderful weather

THE PAINTER

Green trees
Blue skies
Who knew?
That there could be such colors
Surely, the person who painted this
Had an imagination
Where did he find such vibrant colors?
Could such colors ever exist?
The Painter's creativity must have stretched
Beyond the Horizon

MESSAGE IN A BOTTLE
A Short Story

One day I was strolling down the beach when I noticed something shining in the sand. When I dug out some of the sand, I realized it was a bottle. I tried to pull the rest of it out but it was stuck. I tried a thousand times before I got it out. The bottle had a peculiar shape to it. It also had a cork in it. When I opened the bottle, I saw a message inside. I took the message out and it was damp and wrinkled. When I read the message some of the words were smeared, but I could still make them out. The message was a letter sent the year before this year. The message was about two orphans were trying to find their mother. I gave the police the message and they put up flyers. I wrote a message back explaining what I did. Then I threw it back into the ocean hoping that they would get it. When that was over, I went home. This Story was about the day I found a message in a bottle.

The Old Vacant House
A Short Story

Visiting the old vacant house was the best adventure of my life. One day, my friends and I were walking home from school. We came upon an old house that was not ever there before. We were so curious, so we went to look through the windows. We could not see through them because they were covered with dust and cobwebs. The house looked so old that it seemed that if you simply touched it, it would fall over. One of my friends went to see if the door was open. She turned the knob and the door creaked open. She motioned for us to come over through the door. We walked into the house and started screaming because many bats flew out. We went all the way inside. It was cold and dusty. There were spiders everywhere. I walked on a squeaky, loose floorboard. My friends helped me pick it up. When we pulled it back, we noticed it was a flight of stairs. We pulled the rest of the squeaky, loose floorboards back and went down the stairs. As we went down, we saw that something was glowing. We went down farther. The glowing was treasure!

Suddenly, we noticed that there was a skeleton by it! My friends screamed when they saw it. I rolled my eyes at them. Soon, we had gotten over the skeleton and were focusing on the treasure. We held it in our hands. It was so shinny. Then slowly the skeleton rose up! We did not notice because all our attention was on the treasure. The skeleton tapped me on the shoulder. I thought it was one of my friends, so I told it to stop. The skeleton tapped me again. I peeked over to where the skeleton was. It was not there! I whirled around and screamed when I saw it. Soon my friends noticed the skeleton had appeared again too and we all screamed! We started running toward the flight of stairs. I turned back to look at the skeleton. It was a rattling keychain. Then I noticed the stairs were disappearing. I ran faster. I almost did not make it. When we were all out, the stairs had disappeared and skeleton trapped itself inside the house. The skeleton was trying to get out.

We hurried to put the floorboards back. We speedily ran out the front door and went home. We went to find the house the next day. It was not there. It had disappeared! Therefore, we never talked about it again because no one would ever believe us unless the house was there. That was the best adventure of my life.

THE MAGICAL PARK

One day I entered a city park with a lot of swings and slides. It was a hot summer day and I wanted to play. When I turned around, I had seen this park in the distance. I had never seen it before, so I decided to check it out. I ran as fast as I could over to the park. I stopped at the gate. Then, I felt a sudden urge to run over to the sandbox, so I did. As soon as my feet touched the sand, I shrunk into a five year old child. The playground equipment looked HUGE! I was so close to the ground that an adult could mistake me for a garden gnome. I tried to climb the monkey bars but I could not reach them. I tried to slide down the slide, but since I was so short, the slide looked long and I was scared. Lastly, I tried to swing but I could not hop on. Soon I was tired of trying, and just sat on the bench.

A girl walked up to me and started talking. She said, "If you don't leave the park before the gates close, then you will stay five years old forever. That's what happened to me." Suddenly the gate started to close. I was scared. I did not know what to do, so I started running for the gate. Seconds later, I was out of the park, and I had returned to my regular fourth grade body. I went home to tell my mom about what had happened. She did not believe me! I did not try to tell her again what happened because I would waste my breath again. She would never believe me. The day at the "MAGICAL" Park was a day I would never forget!

My Fourth Son

My Fourth Son also has a Biblical name from the Holy Bible. I knew what he would be named immediately! I know that he will lead many in the future to their futures, as he was born a "Leader of Many!" When my son was born, his Pediatrician stated that he had very keen hearing. He loved to beat and tap on things to make noise and dance to music, which is how he received his nickname. This son was very curious at the age of four years old. Not only was he handsome as well, but he was a 'handful' plus some! If anyone in the family said, "Let's go!" he was the first child to find the car keys and was already ready to drive behind the wheel at the age of 4! My fourth son is multi-talented in Sports and Academia! He is very hospitable and self-driven; and seems to stay in high gear. He has a great faith in God. He is learning to become more obedient and get rest to stay refreshed! He is a well-liked, socially talented person, an Honor student, and a new Entrepreneur with his DOBETTER USA Sports Clothing brand. He is a planner, thinker, singer, adventurer, and the center organizer of the party when there is one. He is a true "people person". He loves to travel and loves good quality things. Always remember that GOD directs your Path. He is a very dedicated and loving son who pushes his limits for success. "MAKE YOUR FIELD GOAL WITH LIFE SON!" .....Love Mom

----

Writings by My Fourth Son

INSPIRE FIRE

What is FIRE?

Fire is HOT
Fire does not STOP

Fire is MEAN
Fire quickly comes on the SCENE

What is FIRE?
Fire can INSPIRE

Fire has that red GLOW   ...I KNOW.

THE ROOF IS ON FIRE!

I was in my house

My mom was in a blouse

Everyone was sleep

You could not hear a peep

I was little

I was still counting sheep

1, 2, 3, 4...Here comes the fire knock at my door.

5, 6, 7, 8...I am so sleepy the fire rises from the floor.

Luckily my brother woke up 'cause it was not my time to go
to heaven!

DOGS

Dogs chase frogs
That sits on logs
That you cannot see
In the fog
In the morning
When you like to jog
In that unclear fog
Dogs

SPORTS ARE FUN

Sports like baseball, and soccer, and football are fun
You can play them all day in the sun

Like when you go hunting with a shotgun
In sports all you have to do is have fun

A LIMERICK

A limerick is a short poem with five lines. The first, second, and fifth lines rhyme. The third and fourth lines rhyme. Limericks were first made in Ireland.

THE CLOWN

Yesterday, when my favorite clown arrived
He was wearing a frown
He did a trick
And then, got sick
I am getting a new job in town

I MESSED UP THE FAX!
There once was a boy named Max
Who didn't know how to use a fax
He tried to do it
But he just blew it
That boy named Max

THE LEPRECHAUN

I once met a strange leprechaun
Who was singing on my lawn
When he saw me he stopped
To his knees he dropped
And the next thing I knew he was gone.

FERRIT MOM

There once was a boy named Jarrett
His Mom came from a ferret
She speaks half-bird
And she was a nerd
She loved to eat a carrot.

THE BOY WHO SWALLOWED A TOY

There once was a boy who chewed on a toy
He swallowed a piece
And he doesn't like Kiesh
The boy never had joy

MY FAIRY GODFATHER
A Short Story

Turn the bright lights off! My dog, Rocky dug a deep hole on the beach, and he found a small glowing bottle. I found something jumping like a rabbit in the bottle. It had grey eyes and was wearing a tuxedo and a shirt that was bright red and white with gold and purple wings. I asked him who he was, and he said, "I am your fairy Godfather named Cremson," He then said, "I can grant you one wish!" I was so stunned and confused at that moment. I was happier than a baseball player that just hit a home run. I didn't know what to say. I put the small bottle with Cremson inside in my beach bag and waited until I got home to reopen it.

I hid the bottle in my room until the next wonderful morning. I woke up. It was sunny and beautiful outside. I took out the small jar and I slowly opened the lid. I wondered if my fairy Godfather was still inside. I said are you awake? He flapped his purple and gold wings and jumped up. He asked me if I wanted him to grant my wish now. I said, "Can I wish for anything in the whole world?" He said, "Yes!" My wish was to be the best baseball player ever. Crimson replied, "When you wake up, you will be rich and very famous." I woke up in a three-story mansion with a huge TV and everything! That was my wish. Now I wish that I would have had one more wish.

The End.

My Niece

My Niece, my Sister's Daughter is so uniquely graced and highly favored. She is a Soror who is especially talented in the Arts of Dramatization. She was always naturally drawn to acting and is a beautiful Soul and Honor student who shares her faith in God. Her thoughts are above and beyond. She has grown into a well-rounded young adult leader and lover of mankind with such a genuine smile. My Niece is full of love, and determination! God is on YOUR side. Get ready for the ride. "ENCORE! I CAN'T WAIT FOR YOUR NEXT CURTAIN CALL!"
 .....Much Love to my Niece, Your Auntie Dree

Writings By My Niece

WHAT I THINK ABOUT FIRE

What I think about....
Fire is in the past
It can....
Even break the glass.
My Auntie's home got burned by the

Yes, burned by fire, and now
She is living even higher.
My Auntie needs to try to get more money
Most of all...
... She can still make me laugh. She is still funny.

I THINK

My Niece wrote this beautiful Poem in 2024
For her Auntie Dree

Before the sun rose with its glorious rays,

The little morning star was held captive in space.

An invisible chain had pulled her light years away

From her small, cozy home that had begun to fray.

The chain seemed to tighten the closer the little morning star got

To the giant, dead earth that stood frozen on the spot.

At once the little morning star finally understood her use.

The Commander of the invisible chain wanted to use her as a
    sacrificial flame.

An eternal flame that gives without taking.

THE ADULT'S PLACE

Life highlights the beautiful, the small and the
overlooked moments…

Explore the surviving challenges.

Explore all of the possibilities!

Try something new.

Laugh with a friend…

Feel the warm sunshine, and smell the rain!

~~~~~~~~~~~~~~~~~~~~~

THE ADULT'S PLACE

I have always found a very special place in my Heart for writing during my high school years. My thoughts for writing seemed to flow naturally; nothing forced and I first started writing a few poems in the Bolton High School "Ecrivez". I desire to inspire with the "Fire of a Renewed Spirit" and to fuel those who still feel that dreams seem impossible!

My name, Andrea means that I can be strong and brave. Things are not impossible! It takes time and self-discipline to wait for things to come to fruition, making it harder when you feel alone. I have found scriptural references to what I talk about in my Poems for those who need and love to see the Scriptures. Focus NOT what others may have. Focus on what YOU do have! Focus on those who are around you to help you make a difference in your Family and World. Make something positive happen for yourself today. "FOCUS, then REFOCUS one day at a time!"   .....Love Yourself.

Writings by Andrea

FIRE
WATER
THE SOUNDS

Oh the warm sounds of the crackling fireplace resonating I
    hear
The sound of the jazz, classical wind songs, and the sultry beat
The musical notes rise to the top in the airy atmosphere
Warm water calms my attitude, mood, body, and mind to my feet

Sounds help me drift to another dimension of a tumultuous or
    turbulent time of nopes
The sound of jazz, classical wind sound, and sultry beat
Savors my imagination of sprinting to an era of mystical hopes
Then calms my attitude, mood, body, and mind to my feet

Now the sounds of the whispers are silent
So let my Soul and Peace be still.

It is written, " The voice of the Lord is powerful' the voice of the
Lord is majestic." Psalm 29:3-4 (NIV)

TREES

Trees, trees all around
All your roots are in the ground
You are a part of life and very essential
You bear us fruits and nuts and add more potential
The Earth's purpose of a tree is great
They provide food for your plate
When someone comes to cut you down
Your leaves fall to the ground without a sound
Soon they will rot, be bagged, burned, or bound
Trees, trees all around

It is written, " That person is like a tree planted by streams of water,
which yields its fruit in season and whose leaf does not wither--
whatever they do prospers." Psalms 1-3 (NIV)

SNOWFLAKES

In a world of white, serene, and slow
Snowflakes dance a tranquil show.
Cool beauty falls from the sky
A winter's whisper, a lullaby.

Barefoot steps on a snowy floor,
The crunch of white crystals, I do so adore.
A blanket of silence pure and deep,
In the snowy secret, my soul does keep.

Each flake, a fleeting work of art,
A masterpiece, a frosty heart.
Footprints left in the pristine white,
A dance with winter a sweet delight.

The cold on the skin, a tingling crimson kiss,
Nature's embrace of romance, with nothing amiss.
A journey in the snow so fair,
Leaving memories etched in the wintry air.

...I love seeing the satiny snowfall.

It is written, "Come now, let us settle the matter. Though your sins
are like scarlet they shall be as white as snow; though they are red as
crimson, they shall be like wool." Isaiah 1:18 (NIV)

MY ETERNAL WINTER EMBRACE

In the backyard of winter's first embrace,
Sunshine glistens a tranquil grace on my upturned face.
Sipping from my favorite cup of tea warm in hand,
Nature's symphony of bluebirds has my attention at command.

Snow-kissed branches, a pristine sight,
A world transformed in the softest of morning light.
Wrapped in thoughts of a soft white plush blanket's plea
Here crosses thoughts for warmth all over my body in eternal glee

So wrap me in my beautiful white plush blanket when I die
Yes, in a quiet repose of my final hush, I shall lie
Wrap me in warmth, where stillness flows beneath the cloud
A plush eternal cool clean fragranced white blanket, a tender
   shroud.

As life's flame dims and shadows play
Enfold me gently in that soft array.
Against the chill of endless night,
A cocoon of solace, snug and tight.

Through realms unknown, let my comfort unfurl,
A soft white blanket of love for the departure from this world.
In tranquil slumber, a warmth to find
An eternal embrace, forever kind to my body, and peace of
  mind.

It is written, " Taking Jesus' body the two of them wrapped it, with
the spices, in strips of linen." John 19:40 (NIV)

WALK IN

Walk in the counsel of the wise
Come in and take a seat
Walk in the counsel of the wise
Be open to all wisdom you meet
Walk in the counsel of the wise
Expand your thoughts to critique
Walk in the counsel of the wise
Notice the path of your feet
Walk in the counsel of the wise
Express yourself
Then, change your view
Sit at the feet, meet, and greet
Flow into the brilliant glow of wise wisdom
Walk in the counsel of the wise

It is written: "Blessed is the one who does not walk in step with the
wicked or stand in the way that sinners take or sit in the company of
mockers, but whose delight is in the law of the Lord, and who
meditates on his law day and night."
Psalm 1:1-2 (NIV)

WHEN

When all else fails
When I go through hell
When blessings have poured out
When the miracles removed the doubt

When the chips are down
When the bread bakes brown
When the super is not duper
When the mental state is in a stupar
When the clothes are of holes
When the pipes have no poles
When the right is wrong
When the whisper turns to a song
When the ins turn out
When the cry turns into a shout
When the wet gets dry
When the truth is a lie
When the blind is gone
When the weak get strong
When the sky looks high
When into the night you die
When did you truly know me?
I want to know...

It is written, "There is a time for everything and a season for every activity under the heavens." Ecclesiastes 3:1 (NIV)

TEACH ME

What do you do?
It would be an honor for you to teach me
Teach me how to rock, and roll
Teach me how to soothe my soul

Teach me to love and laugh from deep within
Teach me how to begin and end
Teach me to be slow to speak
Teach me to wash and cook and eat
Teach me to come into the Lord's presence
Teach me how to know another's essence
Teach me, inspire me, and move me
Teach me what you know
I am a child; your child
Teach me
Then, watch me grow

It is written: " Start children off on the way they should go and even when they are old, they will not turn from it." Proverbs 22:6

THE SOUL OF A MARRIAGE

TWO SOULS entwined in the dance of fate,
Marriage is a journey of new beginnings and a wondrous state.
Promised whispers, vows that bind,
In the tapestry of loving hearts aligned.

Together they walk, hand in hand,
Facing storms, on life's shifting sand.
Through laughter and tears a shared embrace,
The symphony of marriage, a lasting grace.

In the quiet moments and lively strife,
They carve a story named "The Essence of Life".
Patience is a virtue, and understanding is key,
The garden of marriage; Love's Legacy.

Challenges met with a united stand,
A partnership forged, strong, and grand.
Each day a chapter, a page to write,
In the book of marriage, love takes a two-soul flight.

Through seasons changing and years that pass,
They find strength in the shadows, through the looking glass.
For in the journey shared a truth unfolds,
Marriage is a tale in the heart it molds.
Beneath the sun's warm and golden kiss,
A marriage, a bond, a bliss.

Rooted in history, a legacy profound,
Love's rhythm, a heartbeat, a resonant sound.
Embrace the past, embrace the now.
A commitment that time cannot disavow.
So, Love tenderly...

It is written, " That is why a man leaves his father and mother and is
united to thewife, and they become one flesh."
Genesis 2:24 (NIV)

THE REALITIES OF LIFE

I walked up to a man with a stride
He gave me a five on the black-hand side
I went to a woman who knew many old remedies
I saw a white man squatting pitching pennies
I saw a young boy running naked in the street
I ran upon a man with corns and blisters on his feet

Around the corner was a man with a gun in his hand;
I asked myself what is to come of this land
While a woman in the narrow street was crying, "Rape!"
A young child was fixing a wound with scotch tape

Little boys in the streets were trying to learn to be hip
Older men lay waiting to prey on them when they do slip
I stared at the police officers having a drag race
Yet when you need them you can't find them any place
Out of all the hundreds of fanatics
I wonder who is, or will become the next drug addict
As I listen to the sound of my heart going "tick-tock
Children are scraping up pennies to buy and share a cold soda pop
When most children should be in school
Many play hooky to go shoot pool
Through all the many toils and strife
These are simply the "Realities of Life".

HE WILL NEVER...THE STILLBORN CHILD

Another child is born of the Human race,
But he will never know the problems he would have to face.

He will never be able to tell a little white lie
Because this beautiful baby will soon die.

Though he is still inside his mother's womb,
His death will come only too soon.

He will never get a chance to see
The lovely things God has given you and me.

This child will never have a chance to live
And find out all the things he had to give.

The baby will never grow up and go to school.
He will never be taught the golden rules.

He will never grow up and fall in love.
He will never learn about the heavenly Father above.

His mother's name he will never know.
He will remember the warmth she gave him, though.

He will never be able to look "alive",
For this baby is a stillborn child.

Who will take pity on this little Human face?
He asks only to be a part of the Human race.
God cares. He will.

It is written, (David speaks after the death of his child): "But now that he is dead, why should I go on fasting? Can I bring him back again? I will go to him, but he will not return to me."

MY JOB IS MOTHER

First, My Job is MOTHER.

Yes, YOU, my children call me "Mother" or "Mamma", not my
    nickname, "Dree!"
You see, I see five little chilrens' staring and lookin' at ME!

I am up at 5:30 AM to midnight, or sometimes till ten o'clock pm.
Just to see that yawl lil chilrens' have clothes and shoes, I ain't got no
    time to visit no gym!

Now, I need yawl to straighn' up! Get things in line cause this is
    School Time made "All the Way Live"!
Let's count one, two, and three... WHERE is four and five?

The older ones have to be driven to their practices here and there
The younger ones are running, and hollering, and pullin at each
    other's hair.
They are All over the house? Believe me I do not mean to swear!
When will the peace of God arrive HERE and with ME stay?
I honestly have only one dollar to feed ya'll today!

Now, I need yawl to straightn' up! Get things in line and done
    cause this is School Time made "All the Way Live!"
Let's count one, two, and three... WHERE is four and five?
It must be God and His angels watchin' over me!

I have managed to go back to school for a better job to maintain.
I have maintained that "A" average in class for little monetary
    gain.
I never thought that I would ever possibly be so good enough to
    pass.
Or have the patience to sit still attending another college for
    another class.

Now, I need yawl to straightn' up! Get things in line and done
    cause this is School Time made "All the Way Live!"
Let's count one, two, and three... WHERE is four and five?

I never imagined I could have so much responsibility.
And have so much possible possibilities to still feel so free.
Yet, this is me.

Now, I need yawl to straightn up! Get things in line and done
    cause this is School Time made "All the Way Live!"
Let's count again. One, two, and three... WHERE is four and five?

Mother I Am, and the Legacy of Mother I be.
I am a survivor. Just turn me loose, and you shall see the true
    ME.

Now, I need yawl to straightn' up! Get things in line and done
    cause this is School Time made "All the Way Live!"
Let's final count. One, two, and three... WHERE is FOUR and
    FIVE?

It is written, " She speaks with wisdom, and faithful instruction is
on her tongue. She watches over the affairs of her household and
does not eat the bread of idleness. Her children arise and call her
blessed; her husband also, and he praises her."
Proverbs 31:26-28 (NIV)

THE LOVE HACK

Love is like a dove
Flying above
Without a shove
Tight as a glove

Of the tingle groove
Ready to move
Nothing to approve
Nothing to remove

Just a constant hug
Snug as a bug
That will escalate
So meditate

Do not hesitate
Or exasperate
If you impregnate
Do not separate

What Doubts? ...You should eliminate
Any debate
Heal, explore, and relate
As you create

And your Souls integrate
Then hearts resonate
To celebrate
Deep Love

Love, Love, Love

That Love Conquers ALL

A BABY

A Baby is full of love and play
One to hold and sing to all day
To snuggle and cuddle
A very, very special thing to juggle

A Baby is a gift from God to bring you joy!

You see its nose, its tiny fingers and toes
You glance into its eyes, yet not its future woes
It's your job to shape and mold
Let the baby have its dreams to behold.

A Baby......A gift from God to bring joy!
Pray, wait and watch.
"Did you know that every good and perfect gift comes from God?"

Eyes that sparkle like a new morning dew
A soul so pure, a love anew
A bundle of joy, wrapped in grace
God's masterpiece, a smooth, giggly, plump tender little face.

It is written, "For you have been my hope, O Sovereign Lord,
My confidence since my youth. From Birth, I have relied on you;
You brought me forth from my mother's womb. I will ever praise
you." (Psalms 71:5-6 NIV)

THE BREAST

The woman's breast, soft as the morning light,
The gentle curves, as delicate as silk in flight.

Tough gravity may eventually pull them down,
They remain a beautiful canvas, so full and round.

49

In youth, they rise like flower petals in the spring,
Awakening a desire, as their silent song may sing.
With age, their story shifts and bends,
Yet grace remains where the form will blend.

To touch is to know warmth, a comfort so deep,
A place where love and tenderness sleep.
Upon this canvas, life begins to trace,
The sacred lines of time and loving grace.

Your man may fall to his knees entranced by their sight,
For in their softness blooms a gentle light.
The breasts are symbols of a woman's soul,
A place where nurturing completes its role.

To signify the maturing of womanhood, as the young girl is fleeing.
A sight that brings delight to her man so pleasing.
A woman's breast has stories to tell,
Nourishing dreams in a gentle swell.

In every silhouette, a sculpted crest
Of nature's quest, known simply as a woman's beautiful breast.
Let them be pleasing and satisfy your special one.

It is written, " A loving doe, a graceful deer-may her breasts satisfy you
always, may you ever be intoxicated with her love." Proverbs 5:19 (NIV)

MY MAN

Look at you. Look at me
Look at you, my Man.

You vowed to stay with me in the still of night...
You promised to be there in the morning light.

Look at you. Look at me
Look at you, my Man

All hopes of tomorrow and yesterday are gone.
What went wrong? I had to leave you alone.

Look at you. Look at me.
Look at you, my Man

You were caught up in the still of night until the daylight.
You got caught up in the black stillness of the city lights and
    the smoke screens in your sight.

Look at you. Look at me.
Look at you, my Man

It makes me choke to see you in such a state. Now, it's too late.
You didn't fight hard enough for me or increase your stake.

Look at you. Look at me.
Look at you, my Man.

Thus saith the Lord to me, "Be free."
There is no more my Man and Me.

Look at you. Look at me.
Look at you, my Man

Your eyes use to reflect a universe of vision for fun and trips
    deep.
In their gaze, I saw promises of love and welfare to keep.

Look at you. Look at me.
Look at you, my Man

Now, your symphony of laughter I shall from refrain,
Your melody that use to soothe me now causes my every pain.

Look at you. Look at me.
Look at you, my Man

Your eyes were used to reflect a universe of vision for fun and trips
    so deep.
In their gaze, I saw promises of love and our welfare to keep.

Look at you. Look at me.
Look at you, my Man.

Look at you. Look at me.
Look at you now. There is no stay for any more romantic getaway.

It is written, "For if you forgive men when they sin against you, your
heavenly Father will also forgive you.
But if you do not forgive men their sin, your Father will not forgive your
sins." Matthew 6:14 (NIV)

NINETY-SEVEN...NINETY-EIGHT...NINETY-NINE
...AND STILL COUNTING

It is written: " Even to your old age I am he, even when you turn gray
will carry you. I have made and will bear. I will carry and will save."
Isaiah 46:4 (NIV)

Well, my GrandMa is in the hospital once more
Her age with pneumonia and arthritis have begun their score.

The dread of poking needles for her nutrients
The loss of oxygen aided the delusions and the do's and don'ts for
   us students.

The telephone calls and visits to be near, to hear her loving voice
   of now
Then the yester years told her, "It won't be long before Jesus
   leads me home, as he will allow."

My GrandMa is a beauty of wisdom wise, full of God's grace
   and mercy
Her nurturing visionary love for the children, and great-
   grandchildren were never a controversy.

Her well-being was well-known by all and I called her a
   "Mother of Many"
Her strength to rear others beyond their birth on Earth was
   a plenty.

The much laughter and the tears we all had for years, listening
   to the ole' stories in the 'White House' on the Hill.
That ole' Indian Hill in Pineville, at 720 Liberia; now Sycamore
   forever remains on our minds still.

Her bowed legs and swollen knee joints have given in to some
    arthritic pain.
Her light brown skin which was so smooth, and soft remains
    the same.
At this age of life, one may wonder what may be gained.
I know she never had a thought about knowing where her
    faith remained

Her life here on this Earth was long to please Him and us,
    which we held so dear.
It was a blessing after blessing, as GrandMa had hung on to a
    love for her own family and Jesus' breath of life from year
    to year.
My heart and eyes feel so full of tears right now...just a taste
    of the faith... the mercy...and the grace.
My GrandMa's stories unfold as they tell about
    the difficulties she had to face.

Yes, the grace of God and so on, and such
The prayer of the righteous does availeth much.
Her journey lasted so long and profound,
A life filled with grace in faith, she is renowned.

To my dear, dear grandmother, Arizona whose heart was full
    of gold,
I love you so much GrandMa with your vast manifold.

Didn't God ask us to taste and see that HE is good?

God did let Ma know what was coming as she stood on
    His Word.
From the beginning, towards the end; the bad, ugly and the
    good she heard.

Her long, thin Indian hair had turned from black-black,
black-gray, and now gray-gray
Her voice would change a pitch or two lighter every day,
and her back now had a slight sway.

My Grandma walked with a purpose as her steps would fleet
Through the bustling years of work and the distant street
Her eyes spoke of tales, of joy and strife
Ninety-eight, Ninety-nine, to almost One Hundred years, what a well-
lived life
What a testimony and still counting.... a memory that will last
forever!

It is written, "Do not cast me away when I am old; do not forsake me
when my strength is gone. Even when I am old and gray, do not forsake
me, O God, till I declare your power to the next generation, and your
might to all who are to come." Psalms 7:19-18 (NIV)

CLOSE THAT DOOR

This relationship is not casual. Listen. Do not talk. There are times when
one person thinks they are right
all the time in their mind. They are not.
I do not want to play that enemy game.
I just want to feel, love, and keep our flame.
The mind is a terrible thing once it starts to think many
wrong thoughts.
Everything does come out eventually.
There are times when one person thinks they are right.
Yes, but why think that... In their mind, but what is their insight?
The most important are the little things that make us tick,
and for our love to stick.
Do not only pay attention to what you see, but to the unseen and feelings
in between.
It is most important that these details are felt, heard, and then breathed
on with closed eyes
Release the mental senses that cause the bad feelings.
Focus on the good good.
Close the door to those spoken ill whispers inside your head
Close that door at once. Open the door to unending and unconditional
Love.

Close any other Door.

The church helps lead you to a true bright
and Morning Star.
To hear and feed on the gospel of our Savior who is very
near and not far.

CLOSE THAT DOOR.

AN ODE TO MY MOM

My Mom is a tall sacrificing, spirited, seeking saint
A symphony of knowledge that will never grow faint
An unhallowed rising sun and beacon so bright
Through chalkboard and pen and Educator with insight

A provider, a positive person of love who helped craft our
    dreams
Her caring, and cautious climb to the top of life's flowing
    streams
With a "just don't stop or give up" attitude woven in time
My Mom is a devoted, full of good deeds, and the
    foundational dweller who kept us in line

A confident, consistent, person who welcomes positive
    change
Her trusted, well-taught teacher of opinionated tenacity
    remain the same

So here's to my Mom whose sacrifice of unfailing love
is profound
Because in every sacrifice her grace is found

Much love to my Mimme whose seeds were sown
My Proverbs 31 Mom you will always be known

Thank you, Mimme.

It is written, "Whatever you do, work at it with all your heart, as working for the Lord, not for men, since you know that you will receive an inheritance from the lord as a reward. It is the Lord Christ you are serving. Colossians 3:23-24 (NIV

THE BATH SANCTUARY

What use to be my motherly "makeshift" toy station for my
kids as their imaginary boat. The boat float has turned into my sensuous
set-up for a constant relaxation moat.
The nighttime segment of routine established, as we step into
the soak of a full warm bodied, tap water infusion with
lavender bath salt. This soothes my soul and love unfolds, as I drift knee
deep into the still calm of a sudsy full warm bath malt.
With closed eyes and the dim light to relax my mind. I have a
sip or two of favoured white wine. I drift into the touch of togetherness
just to soak my feet, legs, thighs, arms, and breasts. To squeeze the
steamy water through the sudsy towel across the nap of my neck, then to
back to my chest. I lift my head and close my eyes again to smell the
steam vapored fragrance of silence to rest, as I wash with the soft cloth
bath towel is our soothing waterpool nest.The sudsy soap moisturizing
my feet to my limbs, as I am open to feel the warm water stimulate my
soft skin running up and down, and in between the members of my
being.

It feels so good to relieve the stress and relax at best before bed.
Relieve my stress. How I love my bath during this stage of life...
as wife. From the years of noisy playtime notion with children in a
bathtub full of toys to this present time with my soap bar of
shimmery Dove or bath lotion. To my time of self-love and love
companionship with my husband. This desire and relaxation with a
sliver of white light and no noise. Just pull the plug, my Love. All the
water seeps down into the drain and the steam seems to dissipate until
the same time of tomorrow.
How wonderful is the seductive silence of my bathtub sanctuary.
Escape to wash away every inch of the grim and grime. Squeeze in a little
lemon or lime.

Spend some time. Release and elevate the mind. Close your eyes
and escape. Start the water, dim the light, and discover your own bathtub
sanctuary. Feel the warm water sedate to reinstate your calm and peace
of mind... "The Bath Sanctuary"

It is written: " Jesus said to him, "The one who has bathed does not need to wash, except for his feet, but is completely clean. And you are clean, but not every one of you."
John 13: 10

THE FULL MOON

One of my favorite astrological wonder
Surely never an ungodly plunder
This golden moon with tranquil glow that soothes us all
Upon the mountains and hill, you do forever fall

The rivers, oceans, and fields must ignite
With all kinds of your ghostly white
In endless dance, you light the way
For dreamers lost or souls astray

The Moon is a timeless org, serene and wise
Reflecting secrets of the open night skies
A beacon in the velvet of the night
Forever bold and forever bright

You hang above as a mystic transformative guide
Oh lovely Moon, you nor we can not hide
You are so round and bright
You bathe the world with your delight
If you do not ask, our dreams may jump over the Moon.

It is written, "Ask for a sign from your God. Ask anything.
Be extravagant. Ask for the Moon!" Isaiah 7:11

MEN FROM KNIGHT TO KING

You are simply so amazing ... You really are
You are born talented; just good ole plain folk

Talented, strong, artistic, amazed to still be alive
King of the "give me five on the black-hand side"

Talented, strong, artistic, amazed to still be walking
King of the "Era of jive-talking"

Talented, strong, artistic, amazed to still be a money-maker
King of the 'taking of other people's things"

Talented, strong, artistic, amazed to still be a lover of helping
    others
King also of "a good deceit undercover"

Talented, strong, artistic, amazed to still be a child of God
King of the "music for the chronically restless" rod

Talented, strong, artistic, amazed to still have a wonderful
    laugh and smile
King of the "make my day or you'll be made style"

Knight, perhaps you have learned the cost
King, your fight is hard to stay righteous but you are not lost

King, God is patient and awaiting your safe return home
Knight, you may still appear to be a fidgety squirm who loves
    to roam

 So "STAND FIRM!" ---When your will is weak
And "STAND FIRM!"--- When your thinking is confused

"STAND FIRM!" ---When your will is weak
And "STAND FIRM!" ----When your thinking is confused

Father of lies can be converted from a Knight to a King to
    remember
Fathers of lies can love others from January through
    December

So Fathers on God's Word, "STAND FIRM!" ---When your will
    is not strong and your eyes peek
And Fathers on God's Word, "STAND FIRM!" --- When your
    thinking is confused and weak

God can make a way out of no way when you have lost
    your hope
God can make you lose your taste for Satan's dope

God will get you out of that deserted dry place
God will make the King rule majestically in mankind's race

It is written, "I will heal their waywardness and love them freely, for
my anger has turned away from them.
  (Hosea 14:4 NIV)

UPS AND DOWNS

I have certainly had my share of ups and downs
With him and without him, and now it is just me around the towns
To this town, that town, which town, and back home again
Now we have one beautiful daughter and four handsome little men

You ask me if I would do this again?
Again?

No job, this job, that job, which job, and where?
No house, no trust, no wishes come true, just a dare
I have certainly had my share of ups and downs
What really matters?.....I sob. I sob. I make frowns

61

Honesty, trust, love, and especially the divine favor from man and
   God above
What really matters? Love, love and more love
Our Heavenly Father, our only true God matters and daily prayer
The never ceasing prayer, as my daily bread to share

Prayer and faith is what I am to be fed with no dare
So, in all things I am thankful and I acknowledge Him as my private
and personal affair

You ask me if I would do this again? Again you ask? Again?
It will be up to God. Until then, I will be happy myself within.

It is written, "What does the worker gain from his toil? I have seen
the burden God has laid on men. He has made everything beautiful
in its time. He has also set eternity in the hearts of men; yet they
cannot fathom what God has done from beginning to end. I know
that there is nothing better for men than to be happy and do good
while they live. That everyone may eat and drink and find
satisfaction in all his toil---this is the gift of God. I know that
everything God does will endure forever; nothing can be added to it
and nothing take from it. God does it so that men will revere him.
(Ecclesiastes 3:9-14 NIV)

A POEM By "Chico" Anderson Wardsworth, Jr.

This is my mom and dad
Their departure from the Earth
Left me and many so sad
I miss my Dad, in many, many ways
But Mom, dear Mom, for the rest of my days
God had mercy on both of you
You suffered not, that he did for you
He knew your conditions
Your time was just up
That's when he stepped in
And brought you both up to sup from his cup

A NEW HEART

God gave me a new heart; the signs are fulfilled in this day
 I was taken from amongst the baggage; taken out of darkness
Now I stand bent head and shoulders over everyone, as I pray

The signs will follow so play your lyre, tambourine, or flute
I was taken from amongst the baggage; taken out of darkness
To do what must be done and speak without being mute

Let the spirit of God fall heavily on the people to rescue you from
   distress
I was taken from among the baggage; taken out of darkness
Continue your prayers; learn right from wrong, then forward
press

With the Lord be faithfully serve him, so you will not be swept
away
I was taken from amongst the baggage; taken out of darkness
Come follow Him, welcome His wonders, and listen as a child to
   what I have to say

He saved my soul and gave me a new start
I was taken from amongst the baggage; taken out of darkness
Beat, beat, beat on so strong my new heart

BLESSED ARE YOU

The LORD of Heaven's Armies brought us back from captivity.
Live together in peaceful sensitivity.
Away from Toil, He gave us Nature; a place to rest.
The God of Israel turned our sorrow into joy. Did you stand the
test?

Look around your town. Did the Lord bless you?
Look around your home. Did the Lord bless you?

Your disaster was deliberately destroyed and overthrown
So rebuild your future by planting and rebuilding what you
   have sown

Have you awakened from the bittersweet taste of sour grapes
Your sleep is very sweet and you wake to see the glistening sun
through the curtain drapes

Look around your town. Did the Lord bless you?
Look around your home. Did the Lord bless you?

As others die for their sins
Your generations of blessings have continued to pour in

Look around your town. Did the Lord bless you?
Look around your home. Did the Lord bless you?

God's new instructions lie deep within your rebirth
Embrace your new journey for a New Testament of self-worth

Look around your town. Did the Lord bless you?
Look around your home. Did the Lord bless you?

HE has scored forevermore as you shed your old self with the
     morning dew
HE has offered a bridge to the divine still traveled by few

Look around your town. Did the Lord bless you?
Look around your home. Did the Lord bless you?

Your ancestors, neighbors, and friends will see and feel God's love
through you
He has shown His face from Earth below and Heaven above –
tis true, tis true

Look around your town. Did the Lord bless you?
Look around your home. Did the Lord bless you?

Go as your sins have been forgiven. Go and sin no more.
Explore your new possibilities in the ash of graveyards, the pits of the
valley, and the lilies in the grass green fields. Go soar!
The Lord has spoken. You are God's people.
                    ~The Lord has blessed you!~

It is written, "The Lord appeared to us in the past saying, "I have loved you with an everlasting love; I have drawn you with unfailing kindness. I will build you up again, and you, Virgin Israel will be rebuilt. Again, you will take up your timbrels and go out to dance with the joyful. Jeremiah 31: 2-4 (NIV)

A PERSONAL CONVERSATION WITH MY GRANDMA

I had a personal conversation with "Ma", my grandmother, Arizona James, who was ninety-two years old at the time. She was the oldest of fourteen children. At that time, Ma had one surviving sister who lived in Tampa, Florida: my Great Aunt Desta (LoDesta) Davis Graham. She decided to come home to live with Ma after her husband Alred died, so she sold her home in Florida. One week later after her arrival to move in with my grandmother, LoDesta went into a diabetic shock, then a coma, then her death. The two sisters had only one week to spend together. I never knew Aunt Desta had diabetes. Shouldn't we all have known that? What are your family secrets? Your health condition should not have been a secret!

All of her brothers are dead. My grandmother had three brothers who served in World War II. One brother served for one month because the war was ending, another trained to be a pilot and later moved on to live in California and became a Pharmacist. My great uncle Benjamin Davis, Jr., known as "Bennie" had the hardest time of all in World War II. According to Ma, he was a truck driver picking up deliveries in Korea. Ma stated the Benny went through a whole lot, and he did not come back home the same from that War. He came back with what she called "shell shock"; a reaction from the War. It was hard for him to sleep. He would hear sounds and shots of the weapons and he would dream of being in the dugout holes surrounded by the dead bodies just to stay alive. (He actually had to do this during the War.) This is what we call a form of PTSD today. Ma's family did not have a TV to see or hear the reports of the War, but they did have a radio. She said it took many months to receive mail from Benny. Many things were hard to get in town.

Real money was not used. Instead, tokens were used to make purchases. The family went without a lot of things in the early 1900's. Ma could not remember everything, but her last statement was, "It was rough!" As small children, Val, Anna and I; the three closest in age grandchildren, would walk up on the streets of Pineville to go to the grocery and hardware stores. I do remember the penny candy we bought at store with the S & H Green stamps to make purchases. Uncle Bennie lived down the street from my grandmother alone in his old age, which was designed like a "shotgun house". One room led into the next room straight back to the back door. Ma would care for him like her own child. She would cook his meals and bring them down the street daily. I would go with her and help, but I mostly would watch and look around the three roomed house. My great uncle Benny is buried in the Veterans National Cemetery in Pineville, Louisiana.

When I graduated from high school after my summer semester in college at LSU in Alexandria, Louisiana, I also joined the United States Army Reserve for six years. I attended basic training in Fort McClellan, Alabama. Yes, I remember crawling on my knees, rolling into fox holes, breaking down a weapon in record time, and shooting the weapon for night fire with green lights flying all around us. This was an eye-opening adventure down my memory lane. Some things are forever embedded within us. All of these experiences add more flavor into our future.

THE FABULOUS YEARS OF 50 AND 60

"A Piece and Handful of Life with Fifty Assumptions and Wishes"

Whose life is this anyway? I will never stop trying to live and give
You a part of me
Being a constant...Hold.
And then,
Hold on a little longer...to make your Mold.
Help me.....Take my hand.... through these Fabulous Years!

- Fear God, breathe, let go and live happier.
- Pray alone or together. It works!
- Live your life. Travel somewhere sometimes.
- Learn to show love.
- Love without fear.
- Love your neighbor, as yourself.
- Love comes back to you even when you let it go.
- I do still wish I could sing. It's better to sing off key than not to sing at all, so Hum. Try Karaoke!
- Apologize, forgive, get over it.
- Show respect not just when it is due, but all the time, especially to elders.
- Pay attention, hear it, see it, smell it, sound it.
- Visit the "Grands" with a smile, love, and hug while there is still time.
- Enjoy sports and stay active to keep yourself alive.
- Stay connected with good friends even across the miles.
- Keep your name and your family name good.
- Admit when you are wrong. Apologize.
- Keep your hands busy so your mind does not wander.
- SEEK NO REVENGE AND HAVE NO PREJUDICE.
- God will speak. Ask him. Say, "Speak Now Lord!"
- Get good sleep to feel refreshed. Cut the TV off. Just Chill.
- Do not go to bed angry. Pillows do not talk. You talk.
- Pay attention to politics early in life, then vote when its time.
- Think about how you spend your time and make the necessary adjustments to spend time wisely.
- Look in the mirror. Watch your waistline, don't let it vanish.
- Do not assume YOU know it all. Give others a chance too.
- Push yourself --- push forward to finish.
- Buy a house. Experience buying a stock to watch it fail or grow.
- Wounds do come and they heal.
- Do not judge a book by its cover. Look inside to see if it is good.
- Do not make someone else look bad.
- Learn to cook, boil water, and season the food.
- Do take time to smell the flowers and the trees and read.
- Plant a garden and feel the dirt of the Earth with your hands.
- Learn to be a "good" parent so your "good" children can take care of you later in life.

- Learn to be a "good" parent so your "good" children can take care of you later.
- Create your own traditions.
- Discover yourself. Work harder at finding your passion.
- Do not let one rotten apple, onion, or potato spoil your bunch.
- Parents, "Ask for help!"
- Smile often, make yourself laugh. Laugh at yourself.
- Make a list and keep a good list of repairmen: appliance men, electrician, plumber, doctors and lawyers.
- Brush your teeth three times a day.
- Good foods for your flesh and bones include folic acid and zinc.
- The trick to sorting socks is buying them "all the same".
- Stay calm during a crisis. Practice makes perfect.
- Do not talk too much. Stay quiet sometimes.
- Learn to ask for forgiveness today.
- Get rid of stuff you are not using. Ask for help.
- It is hard to keep track of lies. They will track you down.
- Always seek more education. It not too late.

THE PRAYER PLACE
Prayers by Andrea

A PRAYER FOR BUILDING

To My LORD of Heaven's Armies and the God of Israel,
You said to all the captives, "Build homes, and plan to stay. Plant gardens, then eat the food they produce. Marry and have children. Then pray for your children's spouses, so that you may have many grandchildren. Multiply! Do not dwindle away! "Do not let the fortune-tellers who are with us in this land trick us. Do not listen to their dreams, because they are telling us lies in God's name, as HE did not send them. God asks us to work for the peace and the prosperity of the city where HE sent us.

Praying to the LORD for the city's welfare will determine your welfare. Oh God's words are truths. The LORD says: "He will come and do for me (us) all the good things you have promised, and He will bring me (us) home again because HE knew the plans HE has for me (us). They are plans for good and not for disaster, to give me (us) a future and a hope. As I continue to read, and read, and reread, and speak, and cry out to GOD, I see, and hear, and feel HIS Word.

Father, in this day I pray, I listen to your message to BUILD. I look for you wholeheartedly, and I will find YOU! Father God, you have sent your Son to end our captivity and restore our fortunes. Bring us home again to our own lands that you promised (Us). Continue to give me (Us) strength to meet these challenges here on Earth. Thank you for speaking to me, oh God... Father
*Scriptural Reference: Jeremiah 29:4-19 (NIV)

OUR HAVRVEST HAS COME!

LORD, WE believe that Heaven's power on Earth is because of our faith filled word. We thank you for our servant that you have brought forth to us by your Spirit, that works for me and my family to bring us into the land of plenty, and to bring our house to its full completion right now, In Jesus Name!

Forgive us Lord of all our sins. We speak to the mountain of poverty, worry, lack, and disbelief right now. And we cast them into the sea, in Jesus" Name. We will not rob God. We will use the word as our sword. Pour out our blessings into our hands, businesses, bank accounts, and through our mail right now.
Pour out your wisdom to us. Teach us how to walk in and manage our abundance. Now, according to Mark 4:26, Lord we have Faith! We are debt free with No bills and No mortgage! You have called all men to give unto our bosom. We give you the glory, Lord.
Thank you, Lord. Our Harvest has come today, in Jesus' name.

Your Children

AFFIRMATIONS

If you ever find yourself not wanting to get out of bed, or alone for any reason, you can feel incredibly powerful once you turn to these affirmations to uplift your spirits and remind yourself or your inherent worth and strength. I have been there. Affirmations are positive, present-tense statements that you repeat to yourself to reinforce an optimistic belief and combat negative thoughts. Be consistent using these affirmations. You will eventually see a shift in your mindset as you build your inner peace and self-love. Play some music you love and dance. Love is on the way. Hold on.
First and foremost, Jesus loves YOU!

1. "I am worthy of love and happiness."
2. "This feeling is temporary; it will pass."
3. "I am stronger than I think."
4. "I choose to focus on things I can control."
5. "I am grateful for the small joys in life."
6. "I am deserving of good things."
7. "I have the power to change my thoughts."
8. "I am enough just as I am."
9. "I am not alone; I have support."
10. "I trust myself to get through this."
11. "I am allowed to take time for myself."
12. "My feelings are valid, and I honor them."
13. "I am proud of myself for making it this far."
14. "I can find peace within myself."
15. "I am capable of creating positive change."
16. "I choose to let go of what I cannot change."
17. "I am worth of self-care and self -compassion."
18. "I am resilient, and I can overcome this."
19. "I believe n my ability to heal."
20. "I am surrounded by love and support."
21." I am in control of my own happiness."
22. "I choose to focus on the present moment."
23. "I am grateful for my strength and perseverance."
24. "I can do all things through God who strengthens ME!"
25. "Jesus love me. Today will be amazing!"

THE PRAYER PLACE

Life is not always smooth…

Poems, Prayers, and Meditation can help you explore surviving the challenges!

Life is full of relationships…

Find strength to hold on to what matters and what is Biblically true with your Faith.

Each handful can help you maintain

and carry HOPE!

My Prayer For You

ANEWED PRAYER
By Andrea

Keep your servant from deliberate sins!
Don't let them control me
Then, I will be free of guilt
And innocent of great sin.

Heavenly Father,
WE thank you for granting us the knowledge of the mysteries of
the Kingdom of Heaven
So that we prosper here on the Earth and in Heaven.

WE thank you that God shall supply all our needs
According to His riches I glory by Christ Jesus
From Generation to Generation, to Generation...

Lord we shall remember that every house is built by someone,
And God is the builder of everything.

WE thank you that we are the House designed and
built by You!

AMEN

May the words of my mouth
And the meditation of my heart
Be pleasing to you.
O Lord, my rock and my redeemer
Psalms 19:12- 14 (NIV)

Lord, you alone are my inheritance, my cup of blessing.
You guard all that is mine.
The land you have given me is a pleasant land.
What a wonderful inheritance.

I will bless the Lord who guides me;
Even at night m y heart instructs me.
I know the Lord is always with me.
I will not be shaken, for he is right beside me.
Psalms 16:5-8 (NIV)

I am praying to you because I know you will answer, O God.
Bend down and listen as I pray.
Show me your unfailing love in wonderful ways.
By your mighty power you rescue
Those who seek refuge from their enemies.
Guard me as your would guard your own eyes.
Hide me in the shadow of your wings.
Protect me from wicked people who attack me.
From murderous enemies who surround me.
Psalms 17:6-9 (NIV)

Arise, O LORD!
Stand against them, and bring them to their knees!
Rescue me from the wicked with our sword!
By the power of your hand, O LORD,
Destroy those who look to this world for their reward.
But satisfy the hunger of your treasured ones.
May their children have plenty,
Leaving an inheritance for their descendants.
Because I am righteous, I will see you,
When I awake, I will see you face to face and be satisfied.Psalms
12:13-15 (NIV)

Amen.

A PRAYER FOR MY CHILDREN

LORD, I pray for my Children. Clear their conscience and give them a strong desire to live Honorably in every way. Restore their sacrifice of praise to you with the fruit of their own lips. Help them to obey their leaders and submit to authority, so that their work will be a joy. Let them not forget to do well, and to share with others, for with such sacrifice God is very pleased. May the God of Peace, and our Lord Jesus Christ equip them with everything good for doing His will. And may he work in them and help them to do what is pleasing to God through Jesus Christ to whom we give the glory. May God be and stay with them forever and ever and ever...Amen. Hebrews 13:15:21 (NIV)

PRAYER BY AYANNA
A Prayer

I pray for God to keep my soul
To guide my life and make me whole

A prayer to keep the devil away
To make today better than yesterday

This prayer I am saying right here and now
Oh God, please hear it and show me how

To love, have joy and peace the same
Lord, if I ever need anything,
I will call on your name

MY FAVORITE PRAYERS IN THE BIBLE

AMERICA PRAY

2 Chronicles 7:14 (NIV)

If my people, which are called by my name, shall humble themselves,
And pray, and seek my face, and turn from their wicked ways;
Then I will hear from heaven, and will forgive their sin, and will heal
their land.

Amen

THE PRAYER OF JABEZ

1 Chronicles 4:10 (NIV)

"And Jabez called on the God of Israel saying, "Oh that you would
bless me indeed, and enlarge my territory, that your hand would be
with me and that you would keep me from evil, that I may not cause
pain!" So God granted him what he requested.

Jabez first asks God to bless him. Second, he asks God to enlarge his
territory or increase his responsibility. Then, he prays that God will
be with him and stay close. Lastly, Jabez asks that God keep him from
harm so that he will be free from pain.

Amen

PSALMS 23

"The Lord is my Shepherd, I shall not want.

A psalm of David.
1 The Lord is my shepherd, I lack nothing.
2   He makes me lie down in green pastures,
he leads me beside quiet waters,
3   he refreshes my soul.
He guides me along the right paths
for his name's sake.
4 Even though I walk
through the darkest valley,[a]
I will fear no evil,
for you are with me;
your rod and your staff,
they comfort me.
5 You prepare a table before me
in the presence of my enemies.
You anoint my head with oil;
my cup overflows.
6 Surely your goodness and love will follow me
all the days of my life,
and I will dwell in the house of the Lord
forever.

CORINTHIANS PRAYER

Colossians 1:1-131
Paul, called to be an apostle of Christ Jesus by the will of God, and
our brother Sosthenes,
2 To the church of God in Corinth, to those sanctified in Christ
Jesus and called to be his holy people, together with all those
everywhere who call on the name of our Lord Jesus Christ—their
Lord and ours:
3 Grace and peace to you from God our Father and the Lord
Jesus Christ.

THANKSGIVING

4 I always thank my God for you because of his grace given you in Christ Jesus. 5 For in him you have been enriched in every way—with all kinds of speech and with all knowledge— 6 God thus confirming our testimony about Christ among you. 7 Therefore you do not lack any spiritual gift as you eagerly wait for our Lord Jesus Christ to be revealed. 8 He will also keep you firm to the end, so that you will be blameless on the day of our Lord Jesus Christ. 9 God is faithful, who has called you into fellowship with his Son, Jesus Christ our Lord.
A Church Divided Over Leaders

10 I appeal to you, brothers and sisters,[a] in the name of our Lord Jesus Christ, that all of you agree with one another in what you say and that there be no divisions among you, but that you be perfectly united in mind and thought. 11 My brothers and sisters, some from Chloe's household have informed me that there are quarrels among you. 12 What I mean is this: One of you says, "I follow Paul"; another, "I follow Apollos"; another, "I follow Cephas[b]"; still another, "I follow Christ."
13 Is Christ divided? Was Paul crucified for you? Were you baptized in the name of Paul?

THE EPHESIANS' PRAYER

Ephesians 1:18-23

18 I pray that the eyes of your heart may be enlightened in order that you may know the hope to which he has called you, the riches of his glorious inheritance in his holy people, 19 and his incomparably great power for us who believe. That power is the same as the mighty strength 20 he exerted when he raised Christ from the dead and seated him at his right hand in the heavenly realms, 21 far above all rule and authority, power and dominion, and every name that is invoked, not only in the present age but also in the one to come. 22 And God placed all things under his feet and appointed him to be head over everything for the church, 23 which is his body, the fullness of him who fills everything in every way.

A List of the Bible Ten Commandments
~Given by Moses in Exodus~
Exodus 20:1-17

1 And God spoke all these words, saying,

2 I am the LORD thy God, which have brought thee out of the land of Egypt, out of the house of bondage.

*1.3 Thou shalt have no other gods before me.
4 Thou shalt not make unto thee any graven image, or any likeness of anything that is in heaven above, or that is in the earth beneath, or that is in the water under the earth.

5 Thou shalt not bow down thyself to them, nor serve them: for I the LORD thy God am a jealous God, visiting the iniquity of the fathers upon the children unto the third and fourth generation of them that hate me;

6 And showing mercy unto thousands of them that love me, and keep my commandments.
*2.7 Thou shalt not take the name of the LORD thy God in vain; for the LORD will not hold him guiltless that taketh his name in vain.

*3.8 Remember the Sabbath day, to keep it holy.

9 Six days shalt thou labour, and do all thy work:

10 But the seventh day is the Sabbath of the LORD thy God: in it thou shalt not do any work, thou, nor thy son, nor thy daughter, thy manservant, nor thy maidservant, nor thy cattle, nor thy stranger that is within thy gates:

11 For in six days the LORD made heaven and earth, the sea, and all that in them is, and rested the seventh day: wherefore the LORD blessed the Sabbath day, and hallowed it.

*5.12 Honour thy father and thy mother: that thy days may be long upon the
land which the LORD thy God giveth thee.
*6.13 Thou shalt not kill.
*7. 14 Thou shalt not commit adultery.
*8.15 Thou shalt not steal.
*9.16 Thou shalt not bear false witness against thy neighbor.
*10.17 Thou shalt not covet thy neighbor's house; thou shalt not covet thy neighbor's wife, nor his manservant, nor his maidservant, nor his ox, nor his ass, nor any thing that is thy neighbor's.

***Another copy of the Bible 10 Commandments, listed in order from Moses can be found at Deuteronomy 5:6-21

"DARE TO STEP OUT"

Hug yourself, and get the courage to step into the unknown, for divine empowerment awaits you! God will empower you to do any job he calls you to do. Challenge yourself. Just dare to believe His written word... Stand firm.

Be encouraged as an individual to dare to venture beyond your comfort zones, trusting in the divine guidance that empowers your journey with joyous enthusiasm.

Speak faith, even when times are tough. Regardless of age, expect the Word of God to happen in your life!

"He that believeth on me, the works that I do shall he do also."
1 Peter 5:6 (NIV)

Andrea's Place

I hope these poems can allow you to delve
into love, friendship, loss, and the many
marks people leave on and with one another!

This "HANDFUL OF LIFE" symbolizes what we
give and take from one another.

I hope these poems and stories will allow you
to follow your arc of life, from the youthful
wonder to the wisdom of older age,

As they reflect and show how each

"HANDFUL" changes over time!

ANDREA'S MESSAGE

Keep practicing loving more and live more for Jesus. Ask God about your situation. Learn about the Holy Spirit, whom Jesus left here on this Earth for us to help lead us into the truth, and knowledge of his Word. Read the Bible for yourself. What have you got to lose? Try reading more each day. Do not get discouraged by being born into the Family that you currently have. Find something good in all the bad stuff to lift yourself up and out, and then help your family and yourself as much as possible. Just do not bring yourself back down in the process!

I AM so thankful for those who have and are continually "sowing seed" into our Family, Land, and New Projects by purchasing ALL my "God Inspired Books"! Other Book titles besides this "A Handful of Life Book of Poems" are "A Fire Arose From My Soul Memoir of Faith", "I Love My Mamma With The Freaky Hair" Children's Book about a Daughter who lives alone with her Mom with Cancer", "CONNECTIONS Until We Part to Another Life"; A Trust and Will Informational Book, "HEALED! A Personal Food, Health, and Medical History Record" with Gumbo and Jambalaya Recipes, with Holistic information plus information about the Slaves and Indians and the foods they consumed, some adorable Themed Pre-Writing and "Tracing Books For All Kids" Pre-Writing Books with coloring items about Earth, Space, the Jungle, and the Sea, and some beautiful "UPCLOSE Journals" for Everyone to write down and share their Memories and Self-Reflections.

These Books will help fund the Family Business ideas, and projects, and go forth to help other Community Charities! "We are to continue to love one another, which is God's highest command!" May you be enlightened by the daily washing of His Word and continue to be filled with all the fruits of the Spirit with evidence and love. We are one nation under God! "May God bless you and may you 'Abound in Abundance.
We do really thank you for reading and purchasing all of Andrea's Books today and sharing the information with everyone!"

AUTHOR AUTOBIOGRAPHY

I can not stop being a Teacher! I am intent on helping my kids, and others' kids learn about LIFE by "Example" whether it be good or bad. It was always so important to show how relationships with others in the classroom should be good ones because you never know what a child must face when they get to their home. Of course, my best advice for Teachers is to establish a "BOND" with their students. Learn to maintain discipline and respect in a classroom first, then seek help immediately from your Administration if you cannot establish discipline on your own! Call Parents! Take a survey of the needs of your classroom students and use that information to your advantage for the Good of All! After 3:15 pm, I first worked and extra job as an Independent Real Estate Agent for Century 21 Erma Adams after hours and weekends. A few years later I proudly became a REALTOR at Lawson Realty, LLC; the first "Minority" Real Estate Agency in Alexandria, Louisiana.

In April 2010, I became Executive Producer and Host of my brainchild – "The AROSE TV SHOW", a new Christian Testimonial Talk Show aired on the new KALB, Channel 2 (5.2) NALB Station. Sponsors and advertisers were needed for this TV innovation to prosper and stay on the airwaves. AROSE stands for A Reproduction Of Saintly Experiences and was managed under (AELLC) - "AROSE Enterprises, LLC.", which was a family operation that first started, and I was involved in teaching my children how to film the Interviews using my cell phone hoping that everyone would learn to use and edit using a software program eventually. AROSE TV was birthed from a vision after the Family lived through a near-death experience, and they 'AROSE' one October Saturday at 2:15 AM from a burning house fire that destroyed everything we had when we lived in a three-bedroom house rental. The children and I were awakened by the smoke filling the air as the curtains burned on the windows.

This experience in their small three-bedroom rental home was an experience that forever changed their lives. The Fire destroyed everything that we owned and held dear. It was hard to look through the charred remains, as our dreams of ever owning their own home went up in smoke as well since we had to recover all of our losses setting us back financially even further. Through this experience of mental and financial depression, the Family we once knew grew into an extended Family of neighbors, the church, the schools attended, and others in their small Alexandria, Louisiana Community, as a God send.

Our expected a Harvest from that experience "in due season" to come NOW as taught in the Word of God! I started writing down my feelings and dreams about my experiences and loves over the years since then. I collected some poems and stories that my children had tucked away inside their notebooks from school. Parts of my first books were lost and erased from her computer by the children because they had one computer to use. One day during the Summer, I was cleaning up boxes of her stored material and guess what; I soon discovered that I had come into my Full Circle Point in Life! I found a few of my old poems, and immediately began writing new poems! Again, although my computer crashed at that time, it was then that I also produced and edited my own short lived Christian Testimony Talk Show with the help of a friend, and her children; THE AROSE TV SHOW in 2010, which was mentioned earlier. This was the 'First Show of its Kind' ever in the Central Louisiana Area. It aired my Testimony with photos of my Family. Look at what God did! He can bring you back to the PLACE and SPACE HE wants YOU to be to CREATE and to BLESS others by providing them with information, so that they can receive the information from just another "ordinary" person like me and my children born into this World!

The importance of relationships established with others on an everyday basis has much more meaning once you figure out who YOU are and who you are! COVID-19 also caused great alarm to everyone. Andrea also had her Aunt Barbara; her Mom's only sister die from COVID-19; she felt that their eyes opened to how God wants us all to love one another NOW while there is still time, and do not forget those who have less. We should always share some of God's goodness with someone, whether it be money, a smile, a meal, a ride, a walk, a talk, a flower, or a note of praise, even with those whom we would not consider our friend or relative...

Yes, even your ENEMY?

After that mishap, she had received an all-expense paid trip to New York to receive a makeover on the Life & Style TV Show, a syndicated property of Sony Pictures. That Show used to air nationally on KAXN, Channel 65, and is currently canceled off TV. Their Family was featured on the Cover of the August 2005 Family Life Magazine. She was so very grateful for her brief time of restoration, but the fight for their financial recovery continued for quite some time. She still had friends and family asking about that TV production who wanted to see the original tapes. They are still waiting on the "laborers and help" to complete the same construction of a brand-new home TODAY, which is another purpose and benefit for this Book by telling and sharing the stories, as God purposed in Andrea's Heart to do! YEARS are nothing in God's Eyes! Continue to expect and BELIEVE!

Although Andrea received an all-expense paid four-day trip to New York for a makeover on The Life and Styles TV Show. The real-life wonders or experience was on her very first episode of THE AROSE TV SHOW, which began on April 11, 2010, highlighting the Testimonies from other Guests in and around the Central Louisiana Area.

I simply asked God what he wanted me to do after having those experiences. I just knew in her heart, and without a doubt that He wanted me to share my Testimony with others. Once HE opened the doors, I eagerly invited others to do the same, as a method to help reach those who did not yet know Christ. "We should not be ashamed to spread the "good news" about Jesus. "We are simply supposed to show brotherly love and tell others of God's love. We are supposed to pray for this Nation and pray that others seek and find Jesus for themselves because there is a Hell! I DO NOT want to go there, nor have anyone else go there!"

The premise of THE AROSE TV SHOW was based on this scripture: John 4:48 (NIV)
"Unless you people see miraculous signs and wonders, Jesus told him, you will never believe."

Right after the SHOW, my children and I started looking for land to build a new home in mid-October of 2005. We soon discovered land was expensive, so we gave up looking for land and resided with my parents. We eventually found five acres near the immediate outskirts of the Lecompte, Louisiana Area. This was a special find for us! After some research about that land was completed, my sister, Anna and I discovered that that piece of land was previously owned by a relative, Claude Davis; a first cousin to our Grandmother, Arizona Davis James. Indeed this land purchase had resurfaced to us through a special deal designed by GOD! See how God works!

We still need to build, but how awesome it was to purchase this beautiful piece of rural green land that they could now see with their own eyes stretching vastly directly off the Highway. "God does a good work in us, and then He works through us to help one another. When we needed help obtaining our own dream goal of having a new home built, we 'AROSE' through many other trials and much more tribulations.

I have a great Faith and will NOT give up! "United WE stand, as we y continue to believe in Jesus!" she stated.

Feel free to adopt my Motto:

"We AROSE and Shine for God through HIS Life Changing Wonders!"

I will not mislead anyone into thinking that everything in their World is perfect because it never has been, and may never be, but they are striving to achieve just like YOU are every day. WE have had emotional, financial, and physical needs that still need to be met daily, but every day now is so beautiful because everyone is ALIVE! WE can ALL smell the flowers, feel the wind, breathe the air, feel the laughter from a good laugh, and feel the sorrows of the great pains of LIFE just like YOU!"

It was such an honor to be able to attend regular church services at The WORD Christian Center in Alexandria, Louisiana back then. She attributes having wonderful Pastors; Pastors Greg and Celeste Texada and a great Church Family who showered the Love of God on all who would visit. This was a major factor in our continued zeal to seek God for themselves with a "go full force ahead attitude." The Church promoted focusing on the Family. The Church had community outreach programs, church picnics, banquets, bible classes, and social events that were needed. They were just one big, ordinary, and modestly happy Cenla Family. FIND a Church that YOU are comfortable with for YOUR Family. Everything is not perfect all the time!   I am no longer scared to ask for help and sincere prayers daily! They love to spend time together. We love to watch movies, football games and occasionally go out to eat together. We celebrate the birthdays. The boys were boys. My Girl was a delight for ALL, especially me and my Grandma Arizona to see! They did not do everything right, like I wanted them to do all the time. The Family loves eating shrimp, crawfish, fried chicken, and fish. As I grew older, I had to learn to watch my salt intake due to blood pressure. I learned to use more digital and computer programs to add to my skills.

I TRULY BELIEVE THAT:

"Children are a Blessing and Education is …
The Blueprint of Life!"

So, get your head out of the clouds and open your eyes.

Take time to Write your Story,

…Enjoy the "HANDFUL OF LIFE" God gives YOU!

85

God had a plan, as long as we can stand the TESTS brought to us while living. Do not give up until God calls you HOME after death! You need your PLAN A and your PLAN B in mind!

My mixed Choctaw Indian grandmother, Arizona "Davis" James raised me while my mother was in college for six years. Arizona (Zona) was also nicknamed - "The Mother of Many", as I called her! "Zona departed this Life on February 15, 2007, and she was one month shy of being one hundred years old. She was also called "Ma" by everyone in the Family. Ma would always press forward daily with a good attitude! Her perseverance is in my genes! Arizona was the last of her fourteen siblings to die just as God had revealed that information to her Grandma in a dream, and Arizona shared with me and the rest of the Family the details of what God had revealed to her. We all lived in Arizona's white wood-framed house originally built by her Uncles Lee and Robert Torry, and older brother, Roosevelt Davis of whom Arizona paid them five hundred dollars to build. They would eat one of her grandmother's home-cooked meals every Sunday in that white house built on "Kinfolk Hill" in Pineville, Louisiana until the last years of her life. The memories of her Grandmother making her fig and pear preserves along with the yellow butter-flavored cake with pineapple preserves on top of the cake gave Andrea the idea for her own ZONA'S PLACE Business, which is a future business opportunity waiting to come into existence again wholly and completely, in Jesus Name! Andrea stated that "their Family needs to seek funds to help keep Arizona's White House on "Kinfolk Hill" restored fully for preservation"! I pray that the funds from this Book will also assist with some of the rebuilding costs to restore my Grandma's House in Pineville, Louisiana today.

We can teach one another to fall to our knees, praise God, and thank him for Jesus, and for adopting us into His family! What does a family mean? Jesus can put out any "FIRE" in your life, as HE is the "Living Water"! Jesus can give you the hope your Family needs. Family means learning to live each day more pleasing to God together through bad times and good times.

A HANDFUL OF LIFE
Book of Poetry

**Published and
Designed By:
AROSE ENTERPRISES, LLC
Copyright November 4, 2024**

**Send the Author a Note
Website: www.aroseenterprisesllc.com**

Email: aroseenterprises1@gmail.com

YOUR PLACE

"A HANDFUL OF LIFE BOOK OF POETRY" is about the moments when your "handful' feels both light and heavy. What would it take to lighten or strengthen your load!

Imagine what it would be like to be able to share your "HANDFUL" with someone else!

What would you give, and what would they take from you?

Fit your memories into the 'Palm of your Hand' and define your moments!

Compare your life to the water, the sand, the new seeds planted, to stars in the sky, or even the thoughts of a new birth, and when you die....

What answers do you have for the what, where, when, and why.

~~~~~~~~~~~~~~~~~~~~~

WHAT IS YOUR STORY

WHAT IS YOUR STORY

_____

_____

_____

_____

_____

_____

_____

_____

_____

_____

_____

_____

_____

_____

_____

_____

_____

_____

_____

_____

_____

_____

_____

_____

_____

_____

_____

_____

_____

_____

_____

_____

_____

_____

_____

POEM REMIX FOR AUNTIE DREE By ABI

Before the sun rose with its glorious rays,
The little morning star was held captive in space.

An invisible chain had pulled her light years away
From her small, cozy home that had begun to fray.

The chain seemed to tighten the closer the little morning star got
To the giant, dead earth that stood frozen on the spot.

At once, the little morning star finally understood her use.
The commander of the invisible chain wanted to
Use her as a sacrificial flame.

An eternal flame that gives without taking,
That consumes without destroying,

That heats without burning,
That dies without living.

Yes, the commander wanted to use her as a sacrifice
To the cold dead earth.
But what is sacrifice without choice?

The little morning star felt her heart scream in pain
And silently wished that she had strong wings to fly her
away.

Far away from the pain, away from the chain, and far, far
away
From what everybody else could gain.

Only the chain remained.
Despite the hope she carried in her heart,

The little morning star never got her wings to fly,
And her light died a little inside.

IN DEATH AND DYING OF A LIFE WELL LIVED
By Andrea

I danced in the morning and I laughed in the night.
I loved with caution and I willed with all my might.

I kissed without counting and I held on without fear.
I lived every moment as though it was dear.

I felt the sun on my face and the wind in my hair.
I loved the thrill of seeing the snow, and the joy of a dare.

I feasted on sunsets and I drank wine watching the stars.
I used my cell phone map and traveled afar.

My hands have known kindness, and my heart has known pain.
I would honestly do it all over, and over again to "love better", as love changes everything with its stain.

For love is the treasure, the prize, the glory, and the key.
The one thing that death could not steal or take from me.

When my last whisper of breath leaves my chest.
I will not clench the hours, or wish for the rest.

I will smile at the heavens and fade with the tide.

For I loved and I lived---Well, oh how I tried!

I may say, "Is this truly it?"

If so, "Can we have a toast to death?" Then, let us stand not sit.

Remembering how we awoke in a place of this era of time and day.

Relax because death will never stay out of your way.

When the alarming clocks helped me to open my eyes.

Remembering the what, the such, and the who, as they did share lies.

I may say again, "Was this truly worth it, and is this truly it?"

If so, I may get mad, I may get angry, so toast. Let us stand together. Do not sit.

We laughed, we made jokes, and how we did sang!

So, think of Life and Death as just another damn good thang!

It keeps you moving forward and wondering...

Who are you to someone else? Who are you?

God made each of us different, especially on the act of faith as we stood.

We get sad and mad, but all these emotions are all good.

We each have our own stories to tell.

Remember, the things you hope to do while living really need to be done well.

The person you strive to be leaves something to give.

The person you strove to be reminds others to continue to live.

I ask, should I have drank more coffee in this life?

Some say that a cup of coffee extends our life with less strife!

If so, let us reach for that cup of coffee to rouse us from this sleep.

Knowing now that I am going to die, savor the love that we need not waste, and do need to keep.

For love, not riches, shine in the end, so I now count the hands that I failed to hold.

And the words left unspoken, because the nights are now turned cold.

Life pours, spills, and washes away, so throw a party at every house and on every block.

Just remember you lived and loved, so praise God you are on His clock.

You must live on to keep on pushing and believing.

You must give honor to whom deserves it, then work, and keep achieving.

Plant me near a beautiful tree and clothe me with my new dressy wardrobe rag.

Sing, dance, and light my grave with my new family designed "Tomb Tag".

I'll not need any riches, or power; just my name carved in stone.

Always remember my presence, and then I will never be alone.

... Receive my Spirit Oh My Lord

...In Death and Dying

~AMEN~

www.ingramcontent.com/pod-product-compliance
Lightning Source LLC
Chambersburg PA
CBHW081154090426
42736CB00017B/3321